ADULT
COLORING
BOOK
FOR
MEN

This Book Belongs To:

_____

_____

Presented By:

_____

Purpose of This Book

This book was created to enable Adults Color in a professional manner, to equip non-artists and open their eyes to the world of art.

"Grown-up shading book for men" isn't simply a customary shading book; it's a novel and connecting with creative excursion planned explicitly for men. This grown-up shading book tries to give men an imaginative outlet that reverberates with their preferences, interests, and remarkable viewpoints. Its motivation is to offer a reviving getaway from the everyday routine, permitting men to loosen up, unwind, and tap into their innovative side while partaking in the advantages of this immortal and reflective action.

Key Targets:

Stress Alleviation: In the present speedy world, men face their portion of pressure and tension. Shading has been demonstrated to be a viable pressure alleviating action that advances care and unwinding. This book intends to assist men with overseeing pressure by giving a quieting and charming experience that urges them to zero in on the current second.

Careful Investigation: " Adult Coloring book for men" highlights unpredictable plans and examples that expect scrupulousness. Drawing in with these plans advances care, permitting men to get away from the bedlam of their regular routines and drench themselves during the time spent shading, cultivating a feeling of peacefulness and mindfulness.

Creative Articulation: Men, similar to any other person, have imaginative tendencies and a craving for innovative articulation. This book perceives and commends the creative side of men, giving them a stage to articulate their thoughts through varieties, concealing, and individual translations of each plan.

Gender-Inclusive: While this shading book is custom-made to men's inclinations, it invites any individual who values its subjects and plans. It challenges conventional orientation generalizations by displaying a great many subjects, from nature and mathematical examples to extract craftsmanship, guaranteeing that everybody can find something that impacts them.

Side interests and Relaxation: " Recognized Manifestations" gives an astounding leisure activity to men to enjoy during their recreation time. It's an extraordinary method for detaching from screens, loosen up, and take part in a fantastic, non-serious movement that supports imagination.

Restorative Advantages: Shading has restorative characteristics, further developing concentration, dexterity, and advancing a feeling of achievement as each page shows signs of life with colors. This book expects to upgrade these helpful advantages, emphatically influencing men's general prosperity.

"Adult Coloring book for men" isn't simply a shading book; it's a careful and comprehensive space where men can investigate their imagination, ease pressure, and track down comfort in the realm of craftsmanship. It empowers a fair and upbeat life by embracing the straightforward joy of shading while at the same time praising the multi-layered nature of manliness.

The Journey Begins

HERE

QUOTE FOR THE DAY

Take up one idea. Make that one idea your life - think of it, dream of it, live on that idea. Let the brain, muscles, nerves, every part of your body, be full of that idea, and just leave every other idea alone. This is the way to success.

Swami Vivekananda

If you hear a voice within you say 'you cannot paint,' then by all means paint, and that voice will be silenced.

Vincent Van Gogh

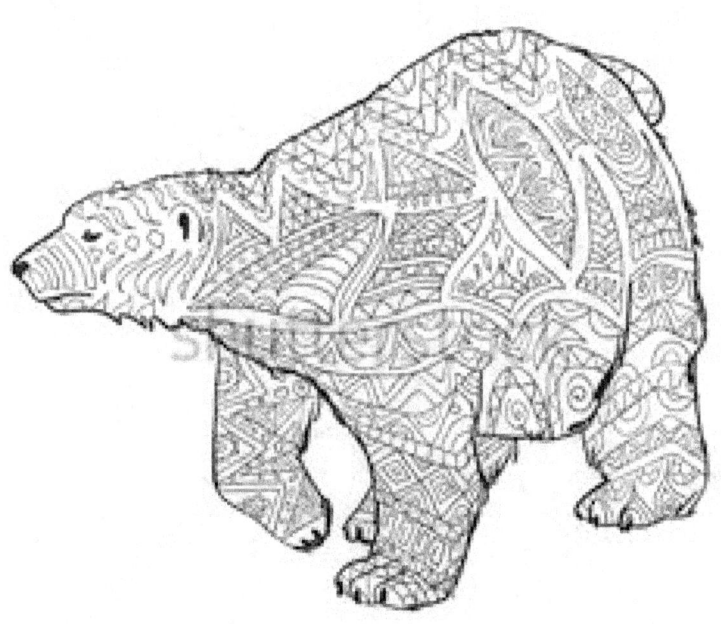

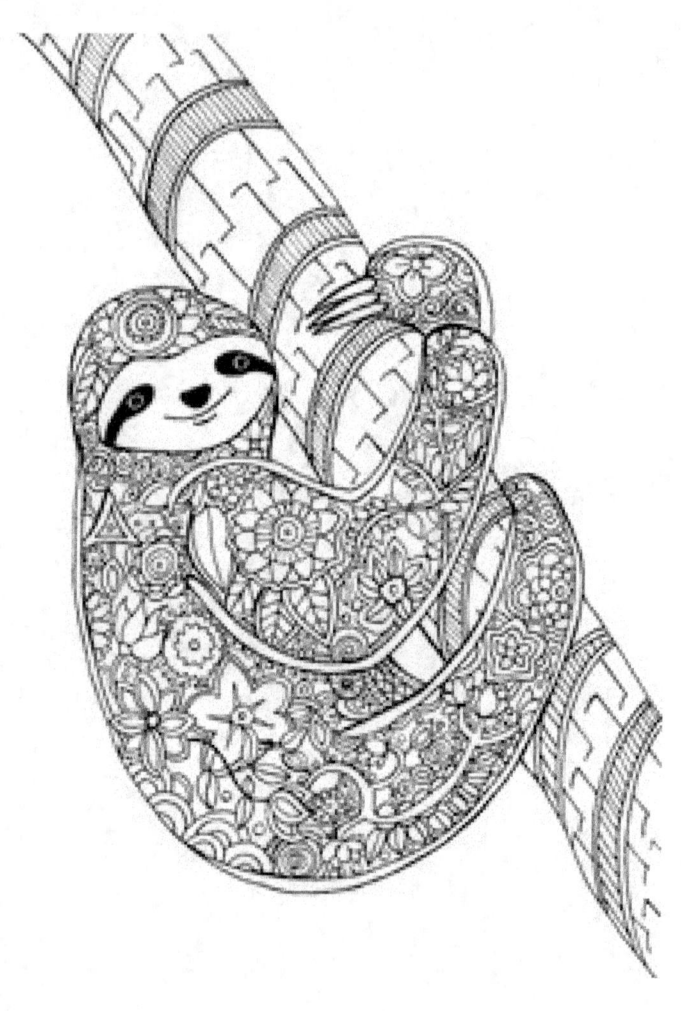

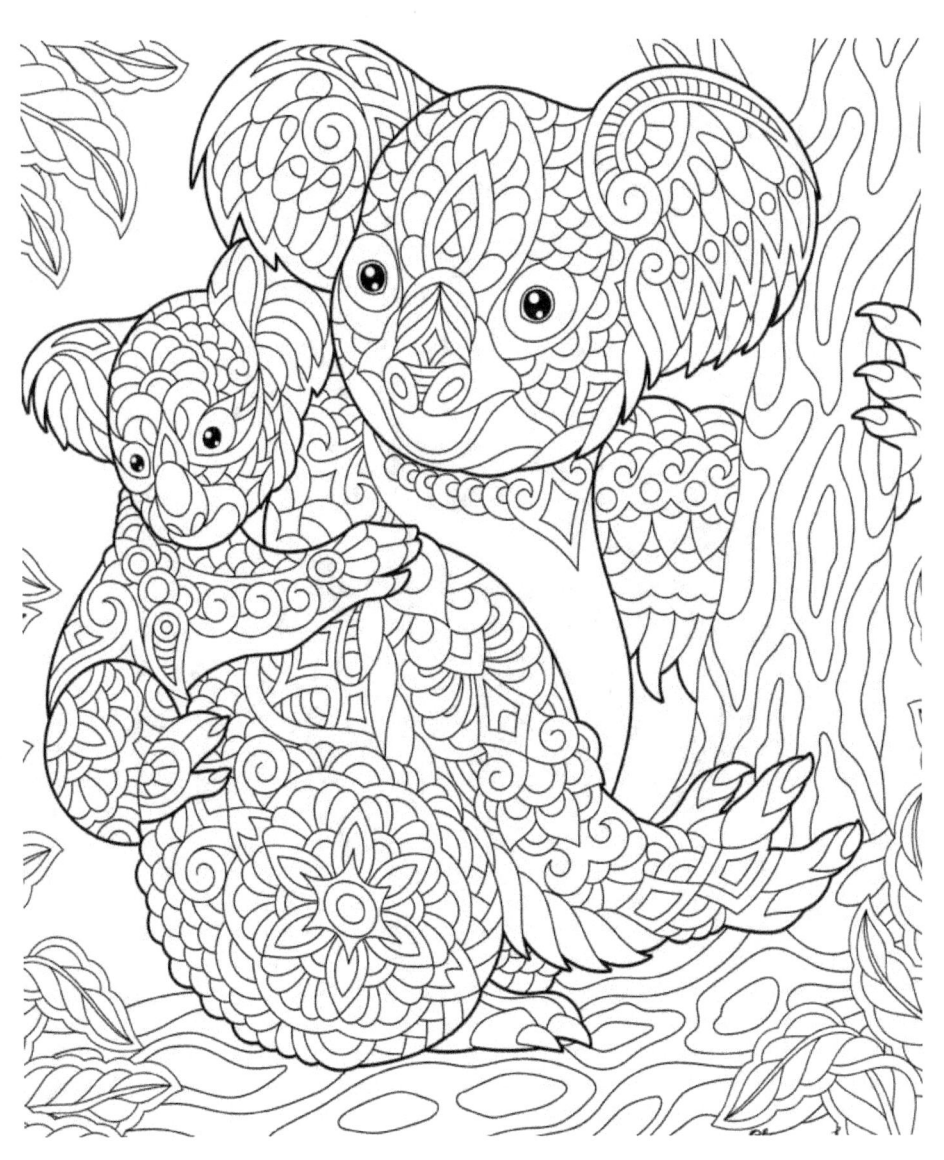

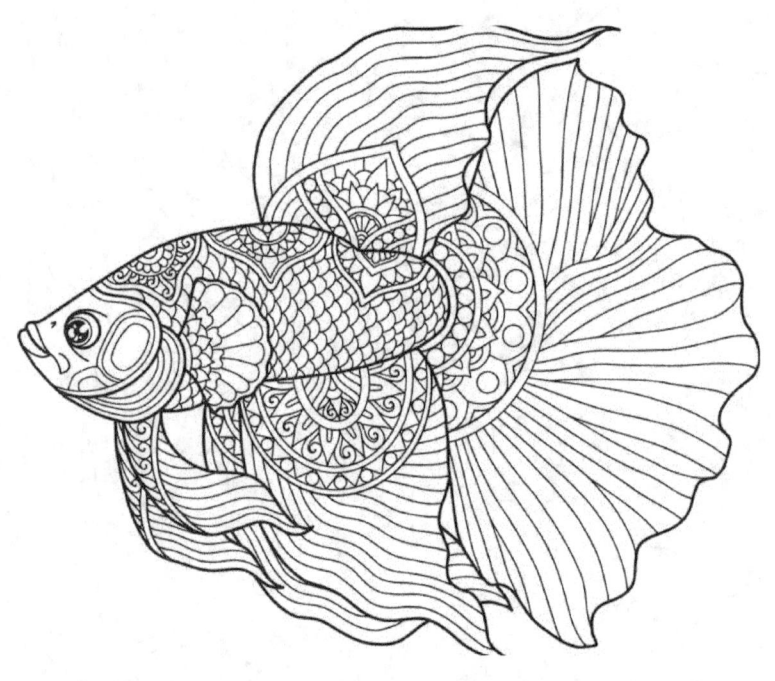

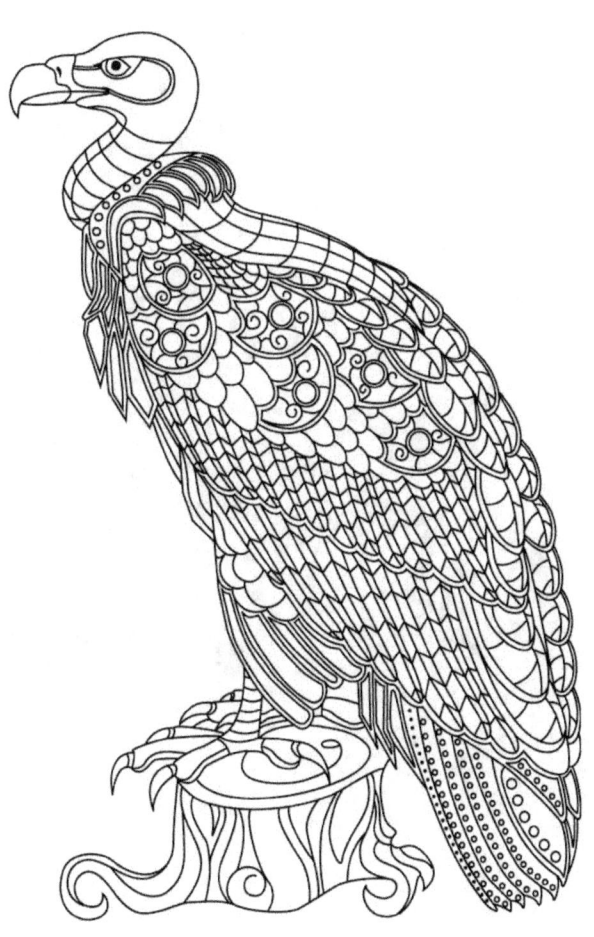

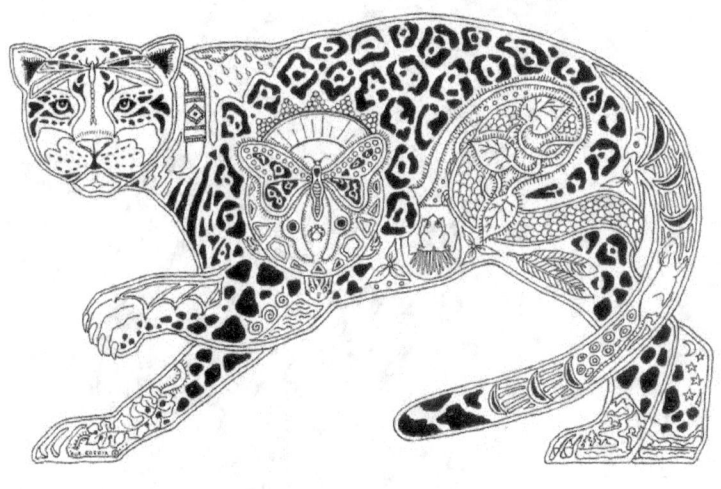

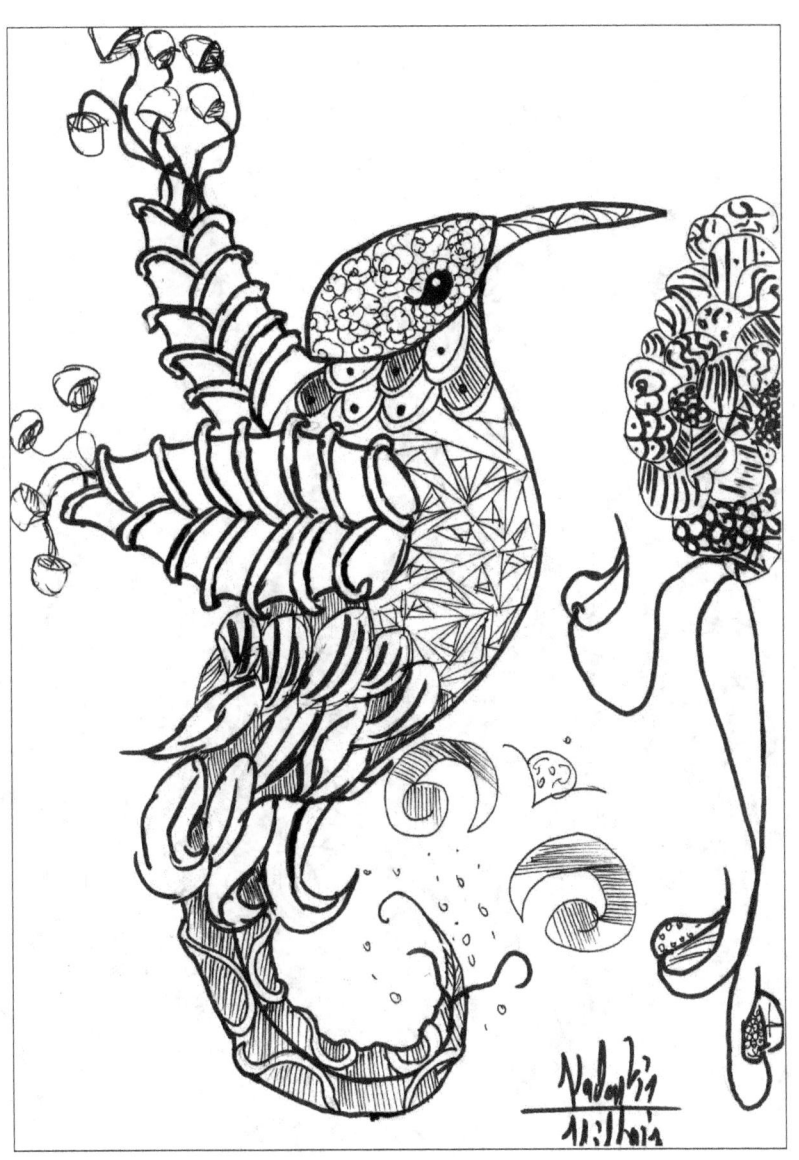

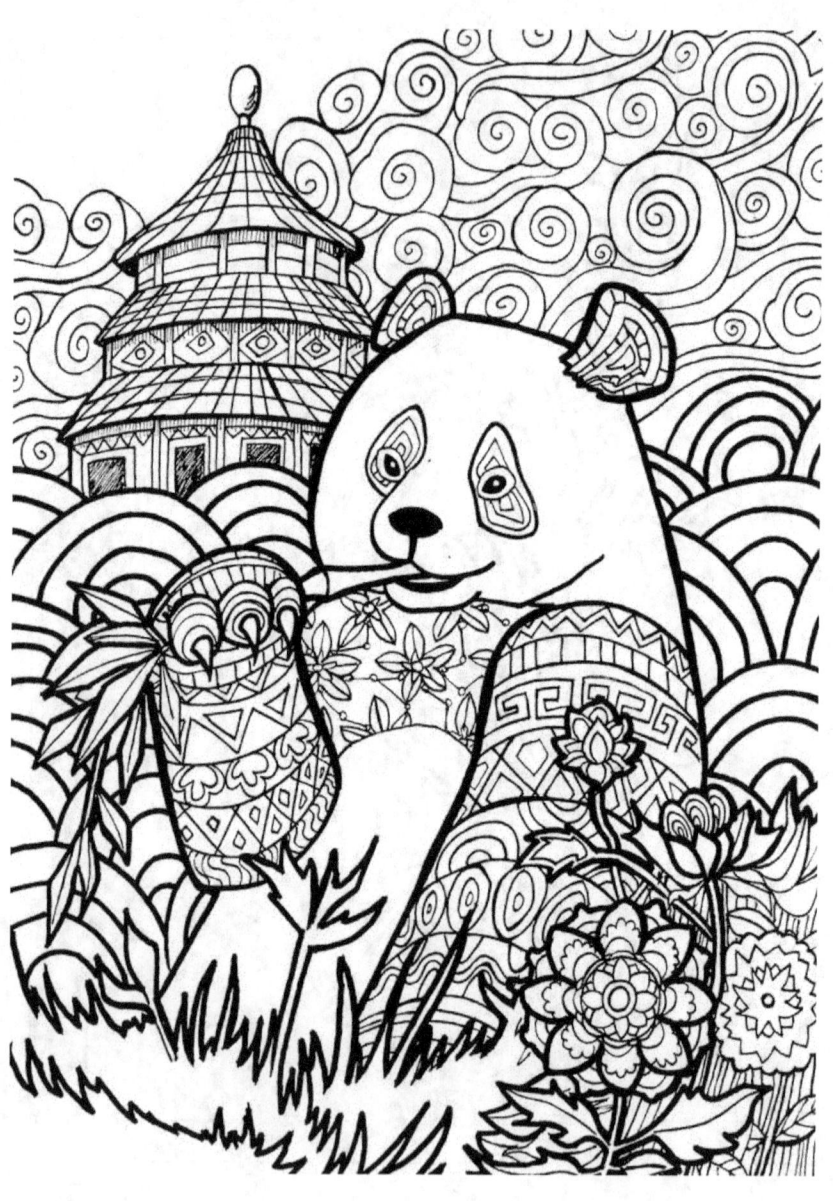

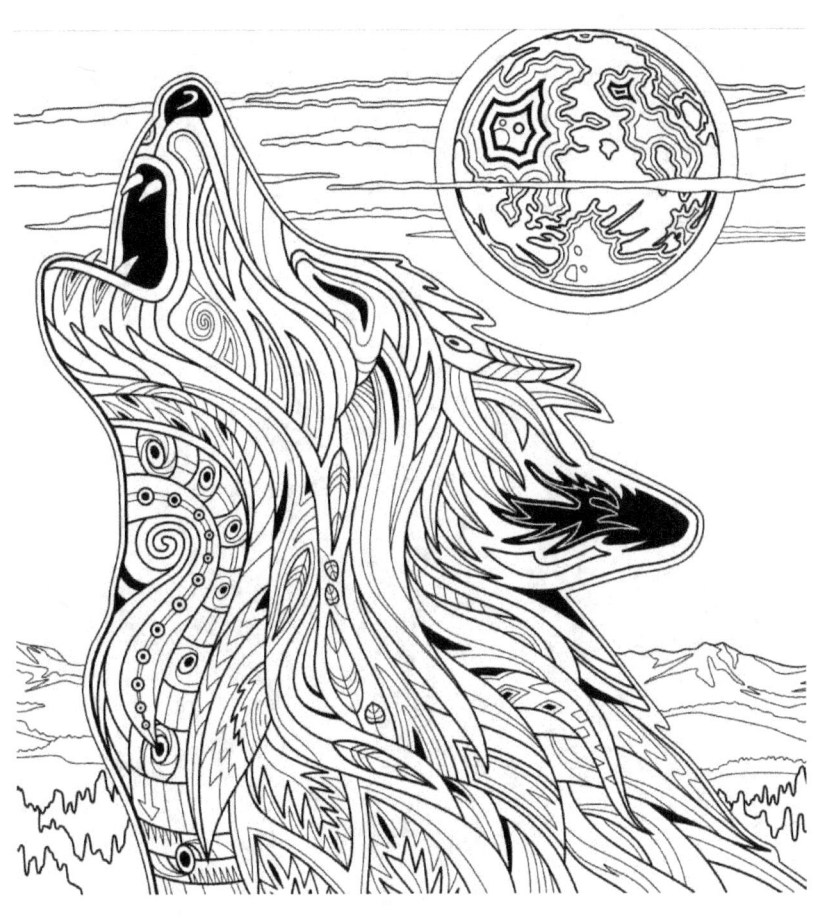

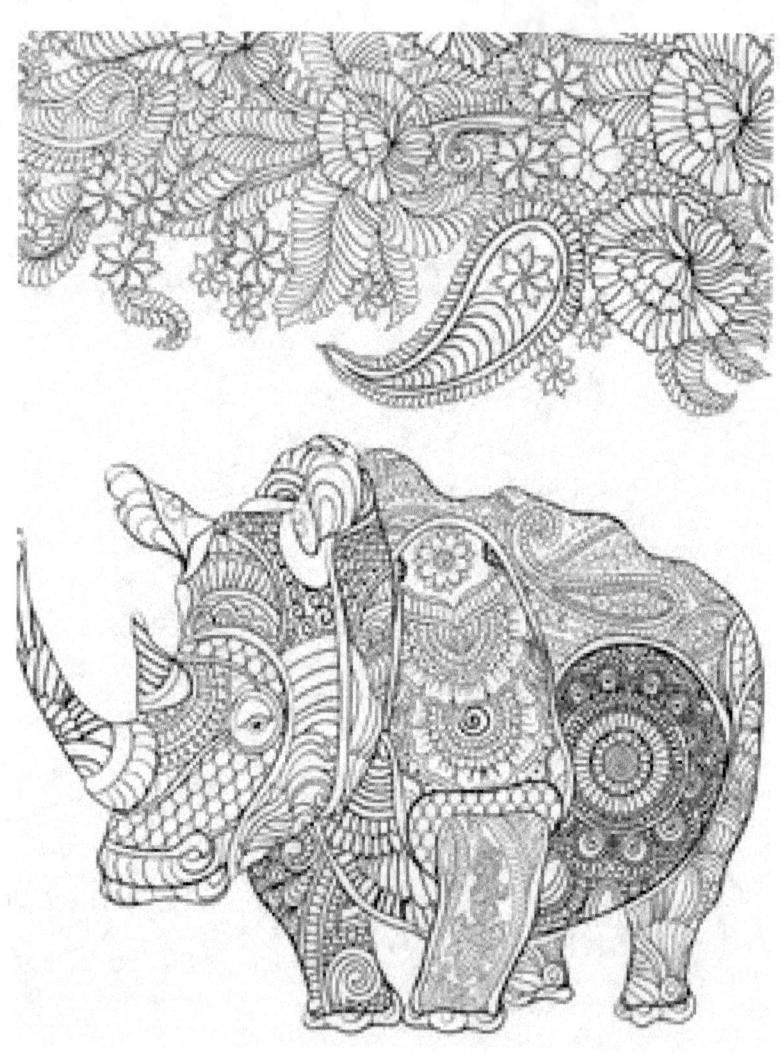

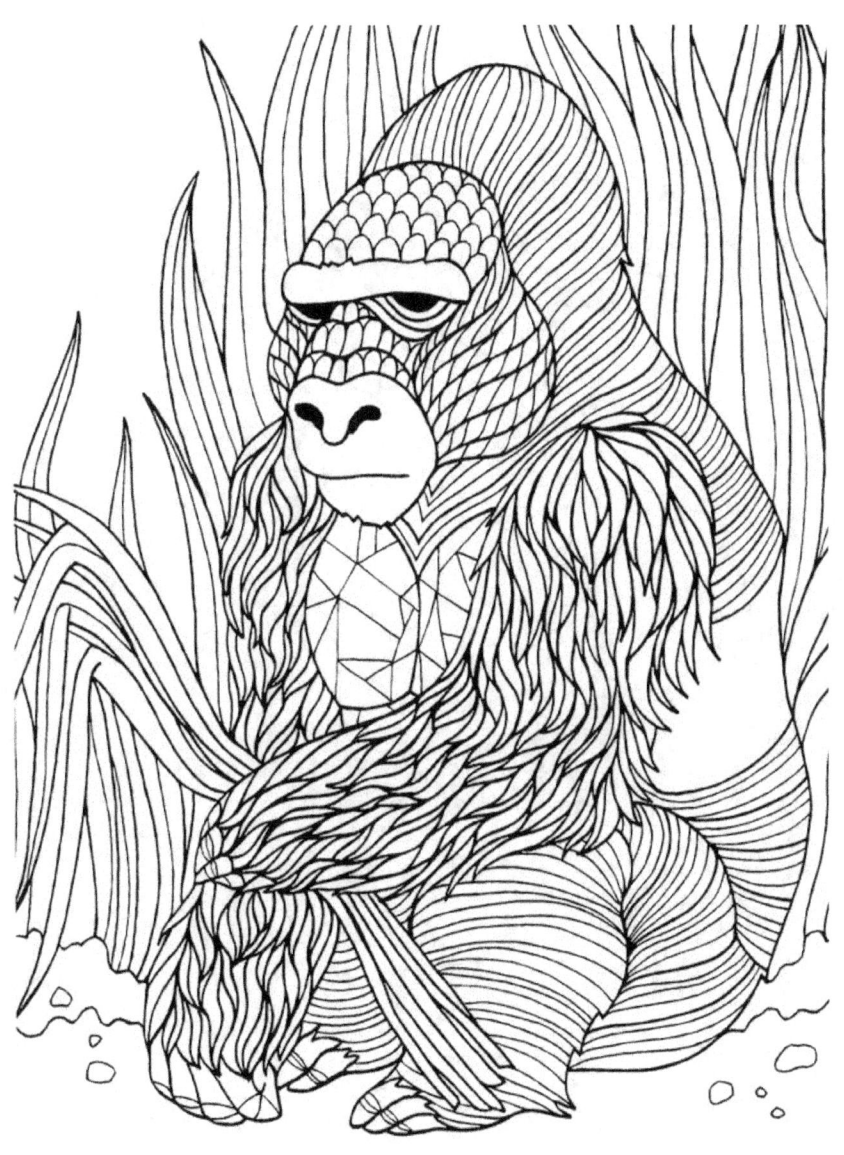

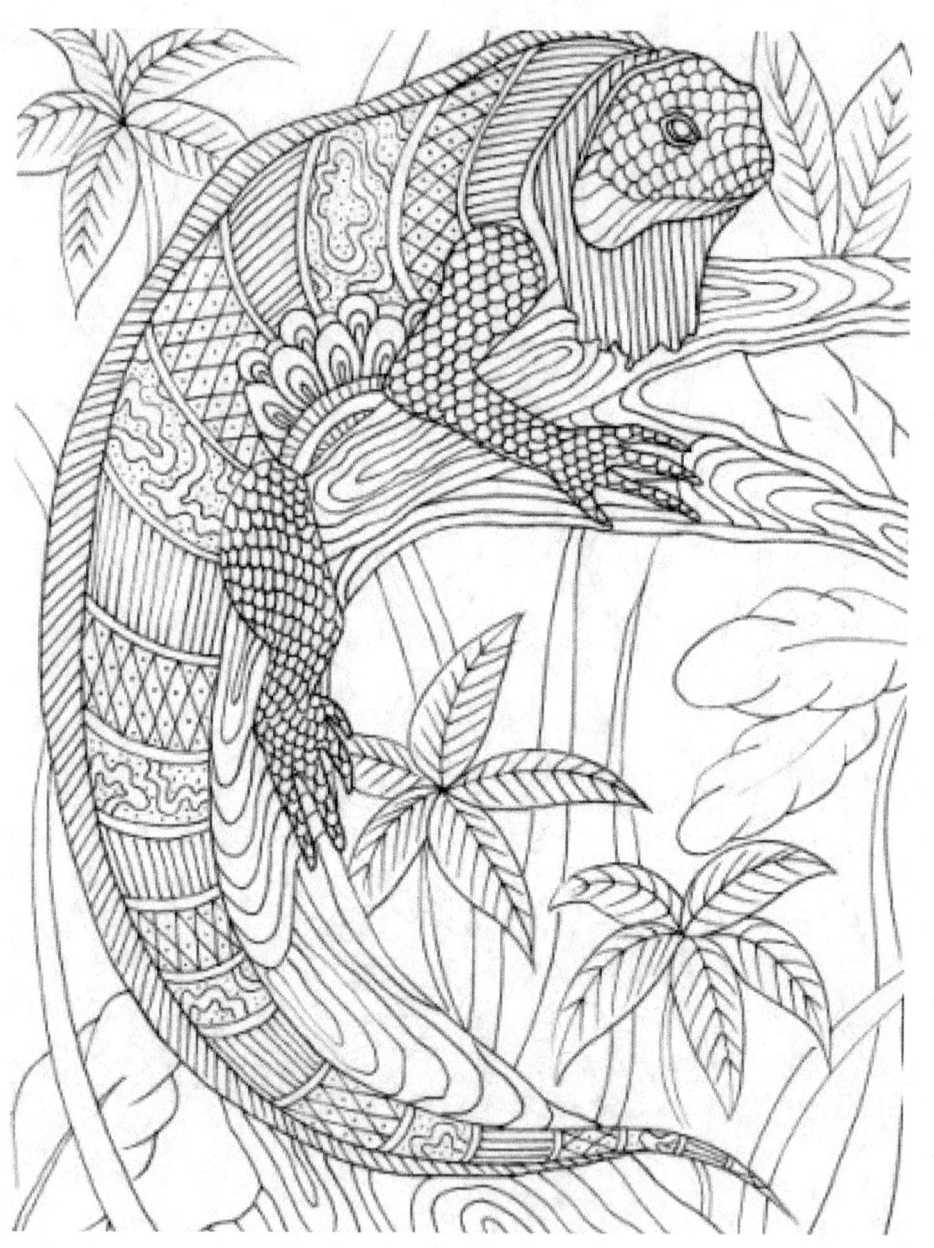

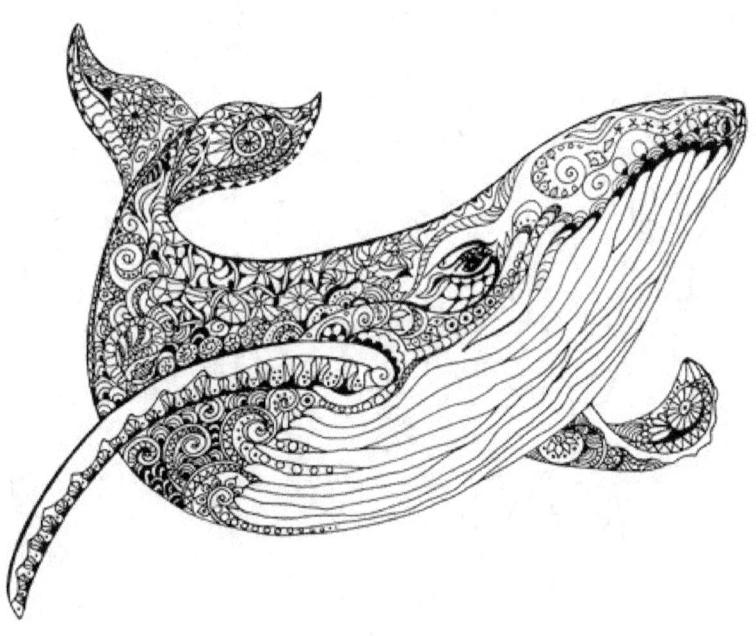

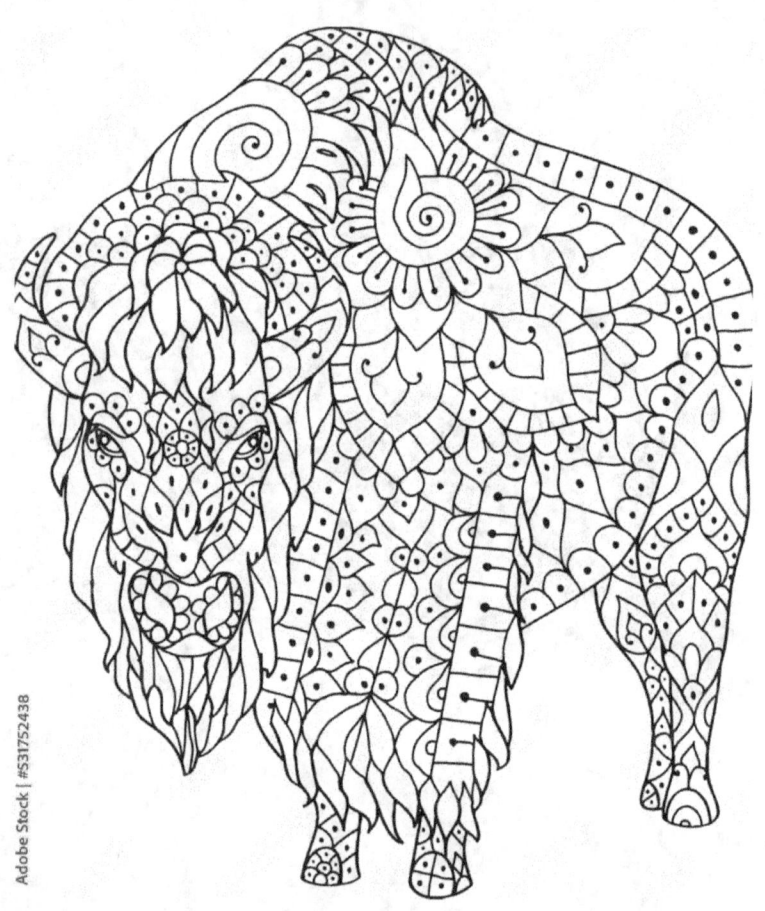

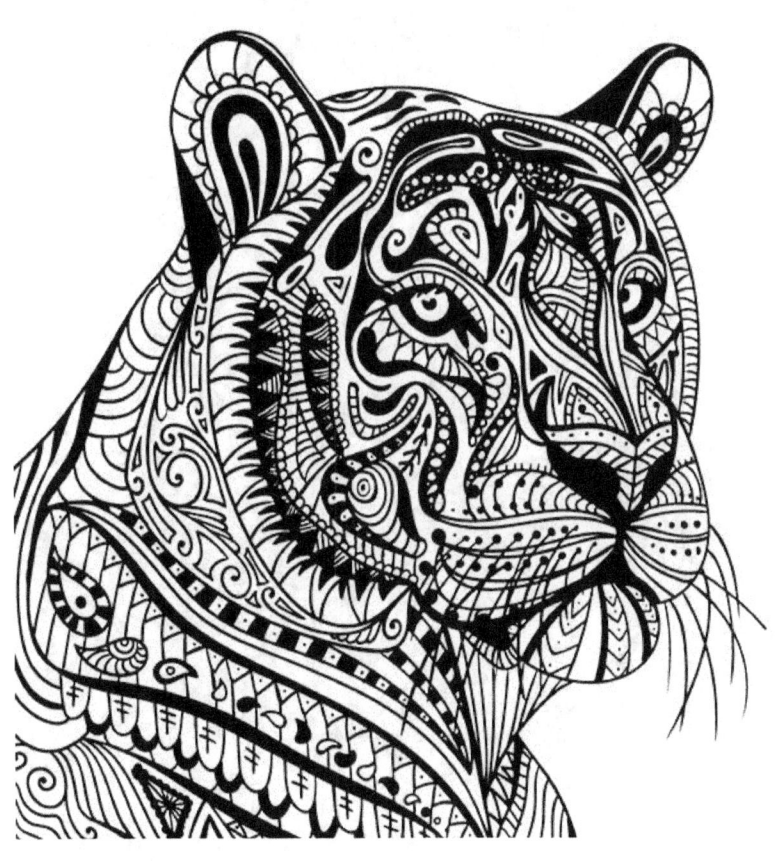

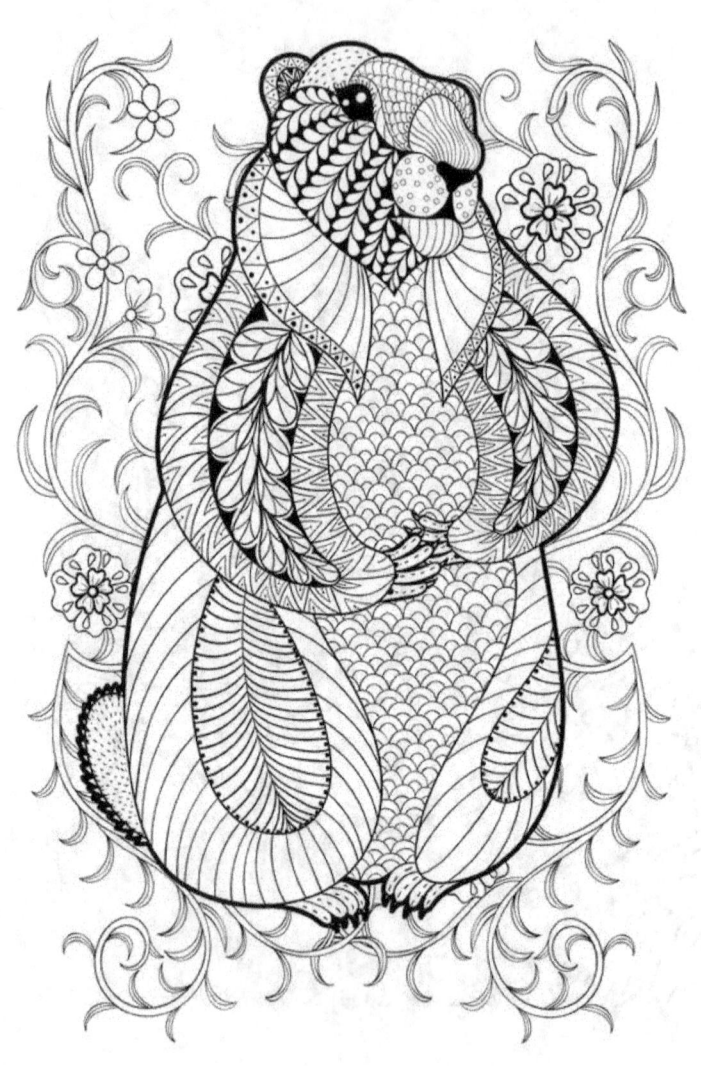

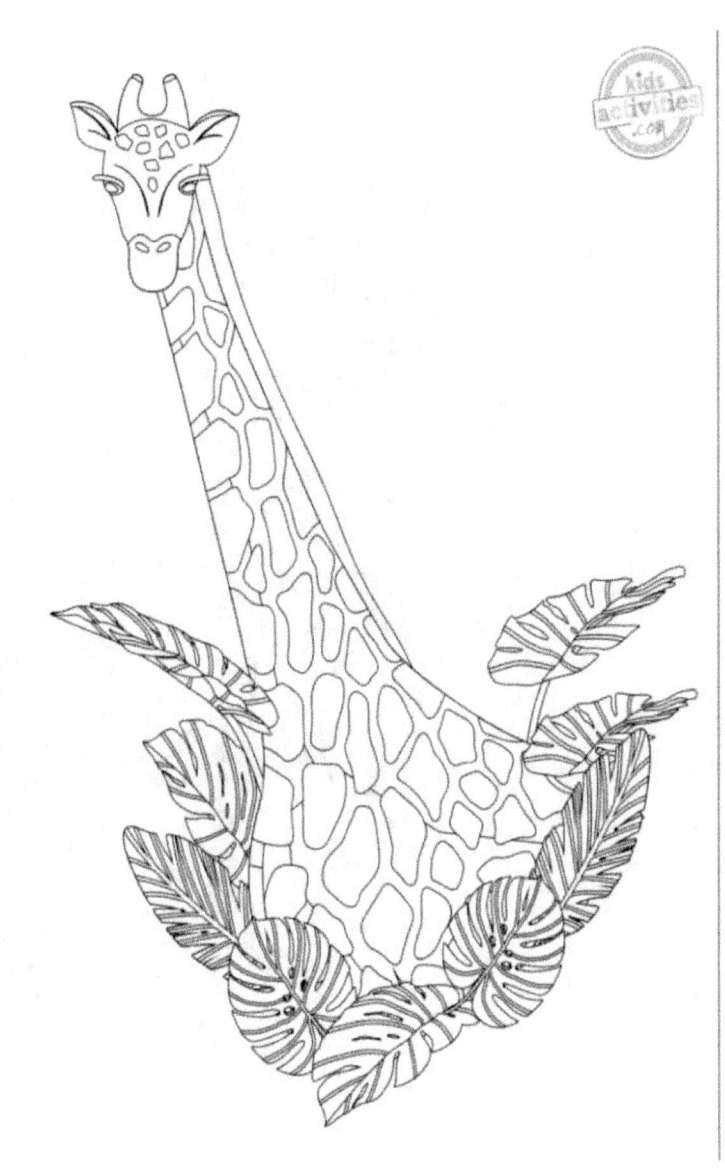

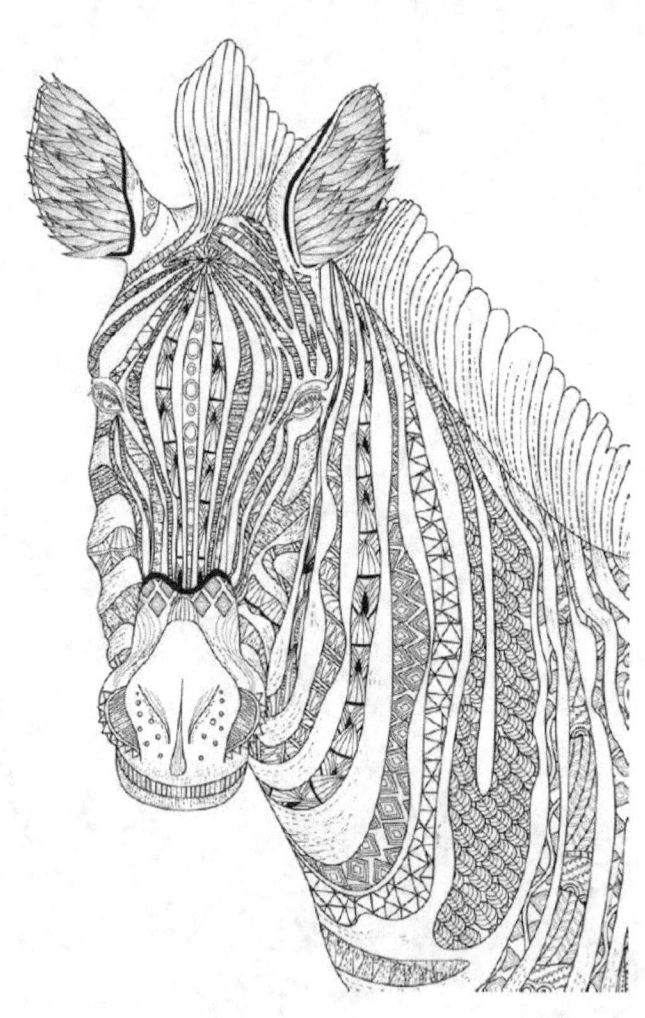

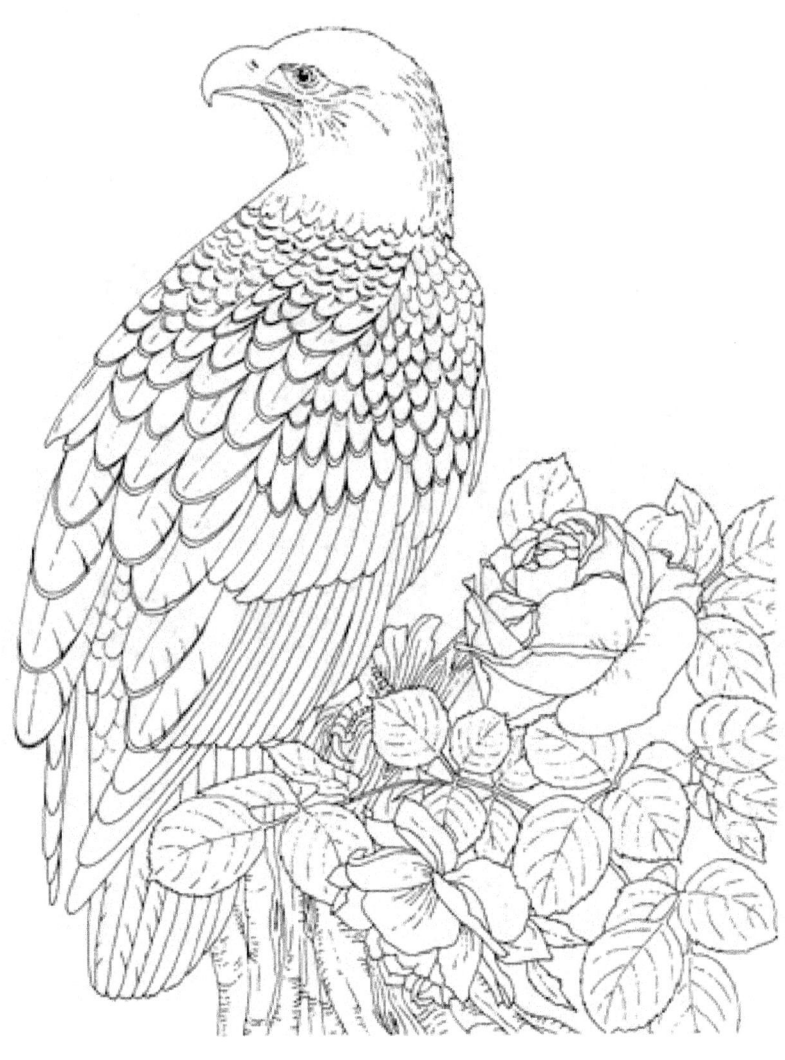

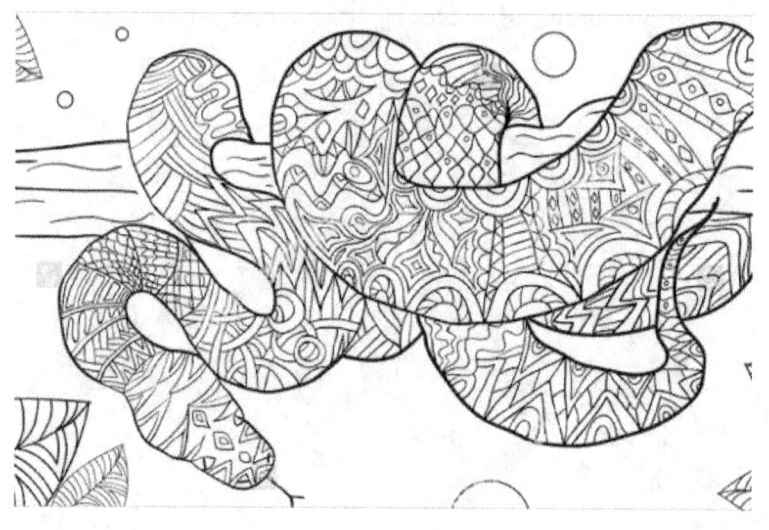

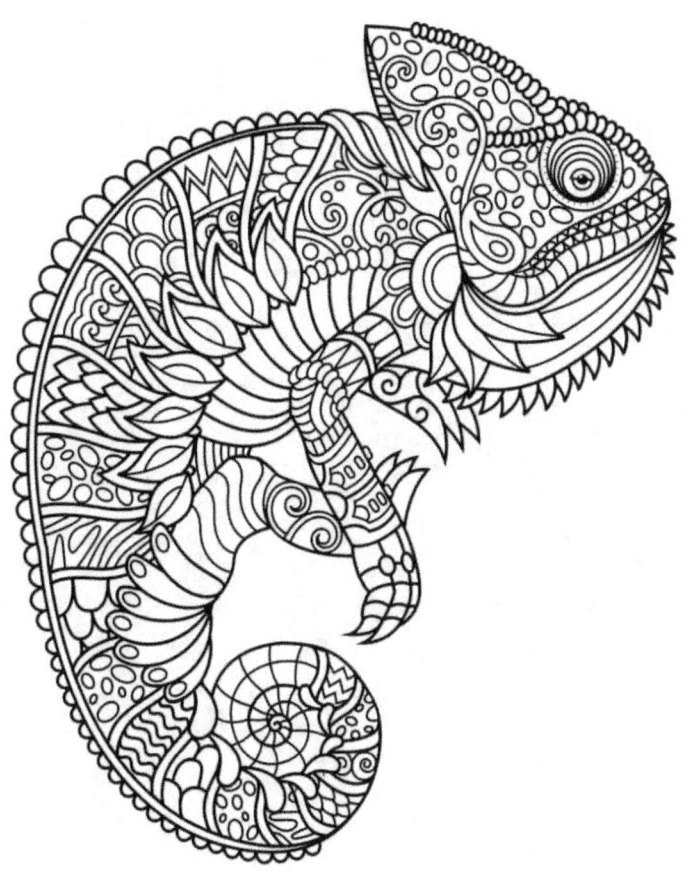

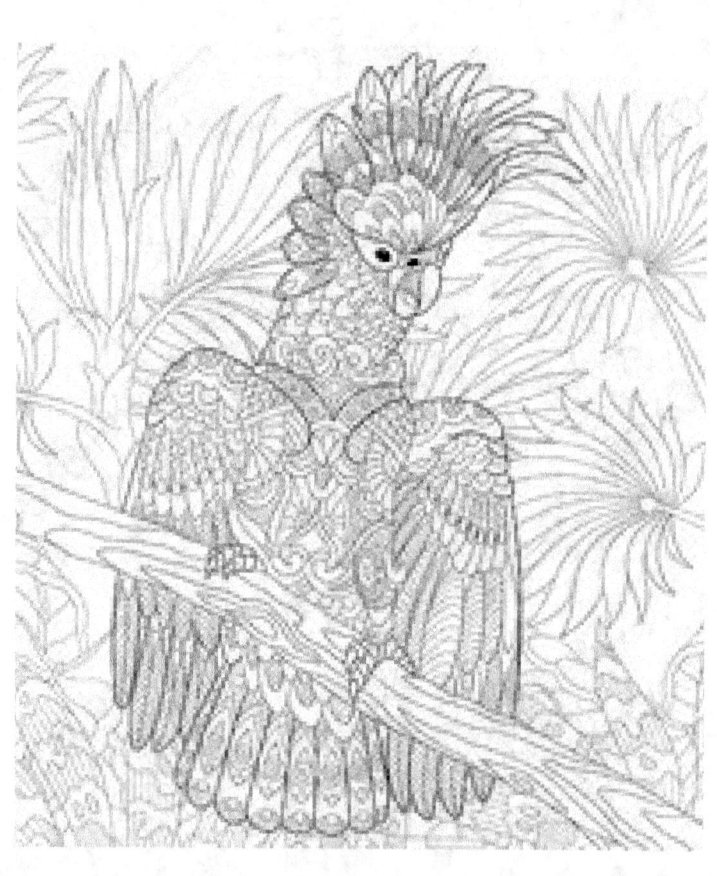

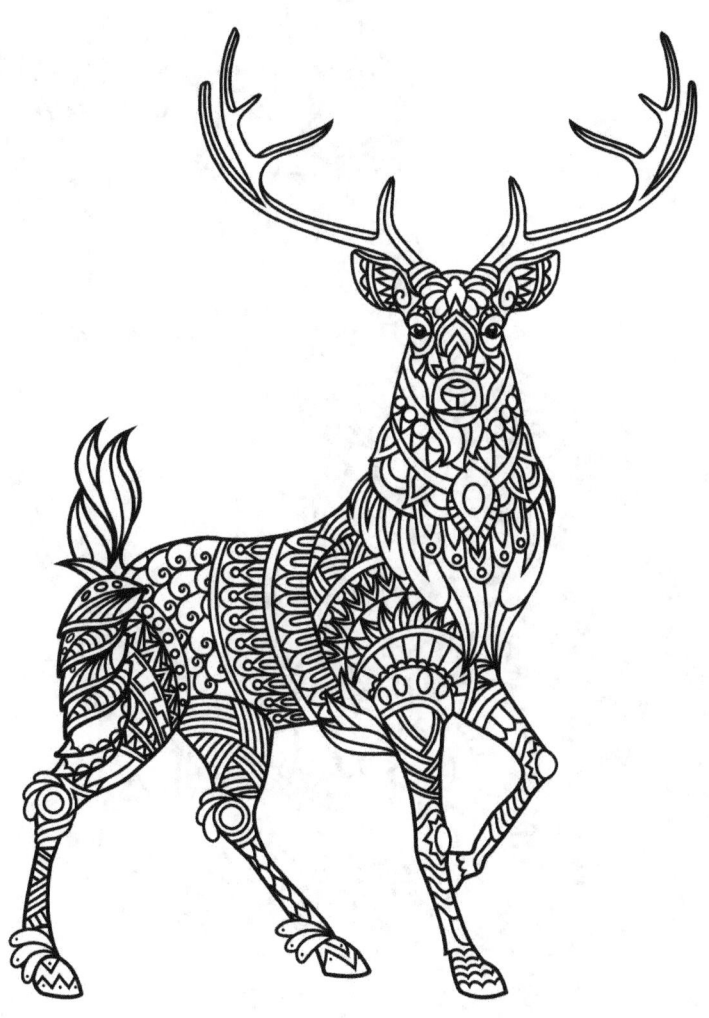

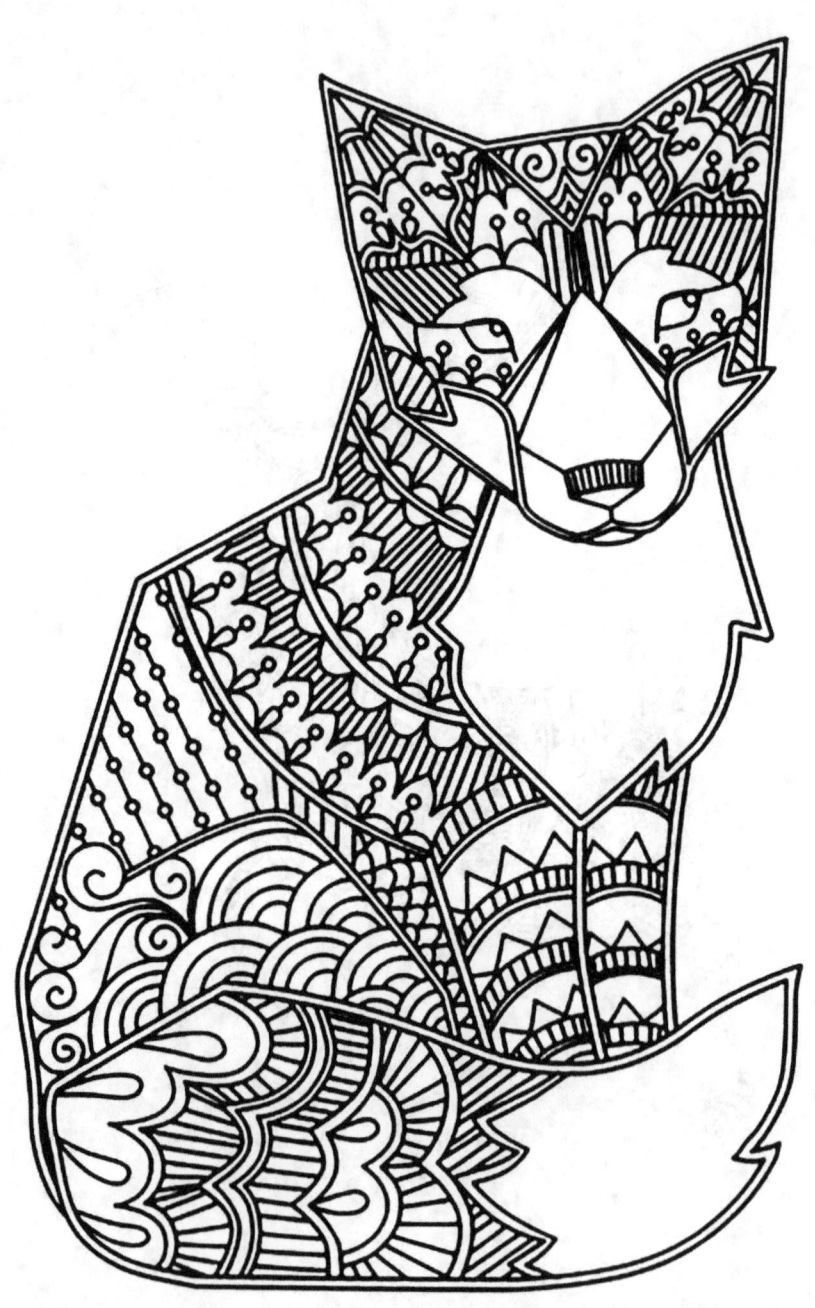

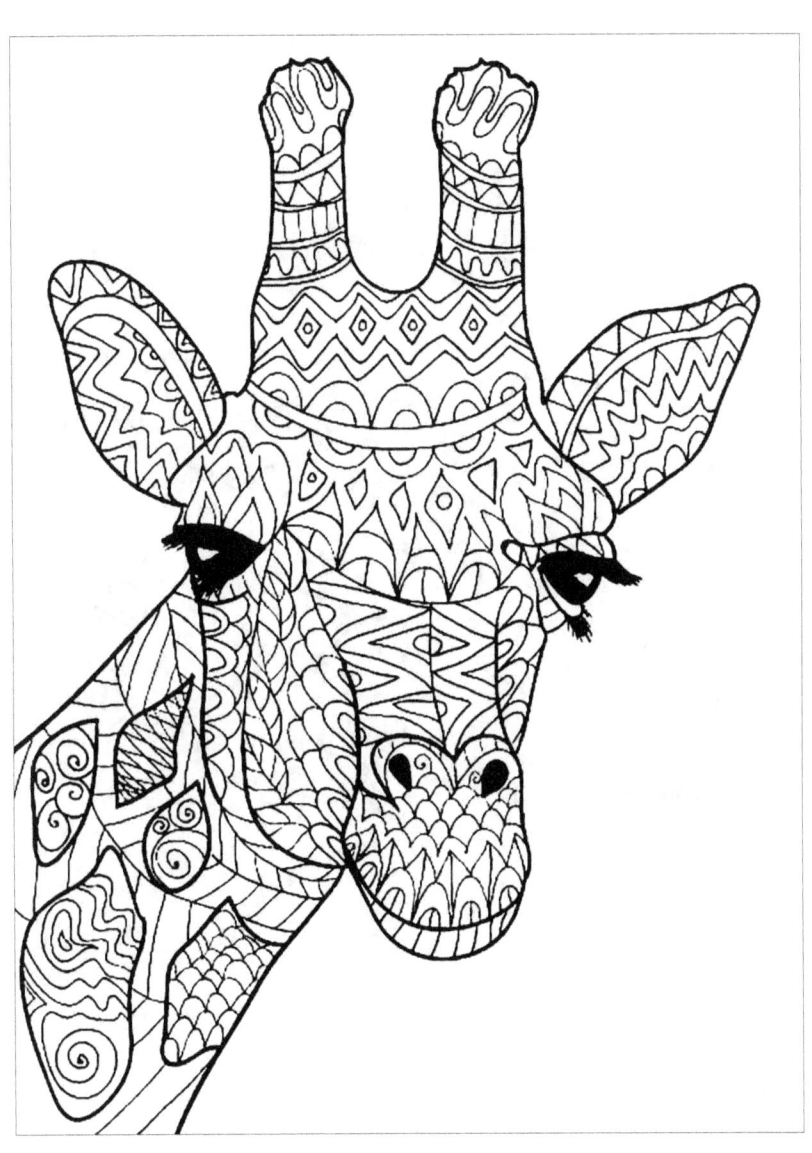

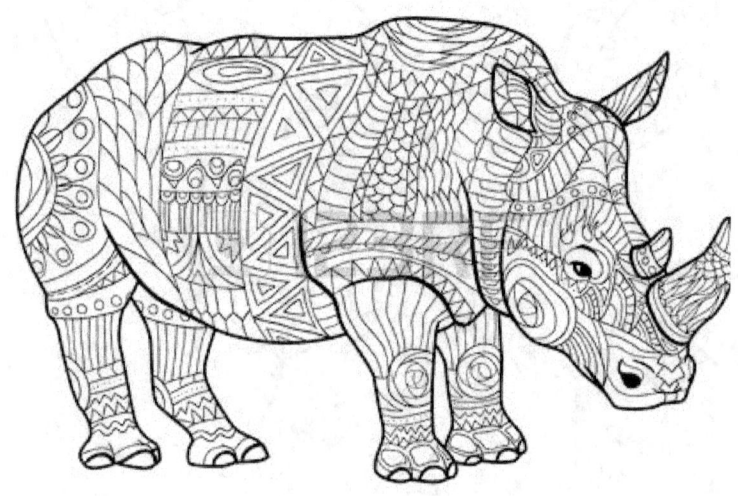

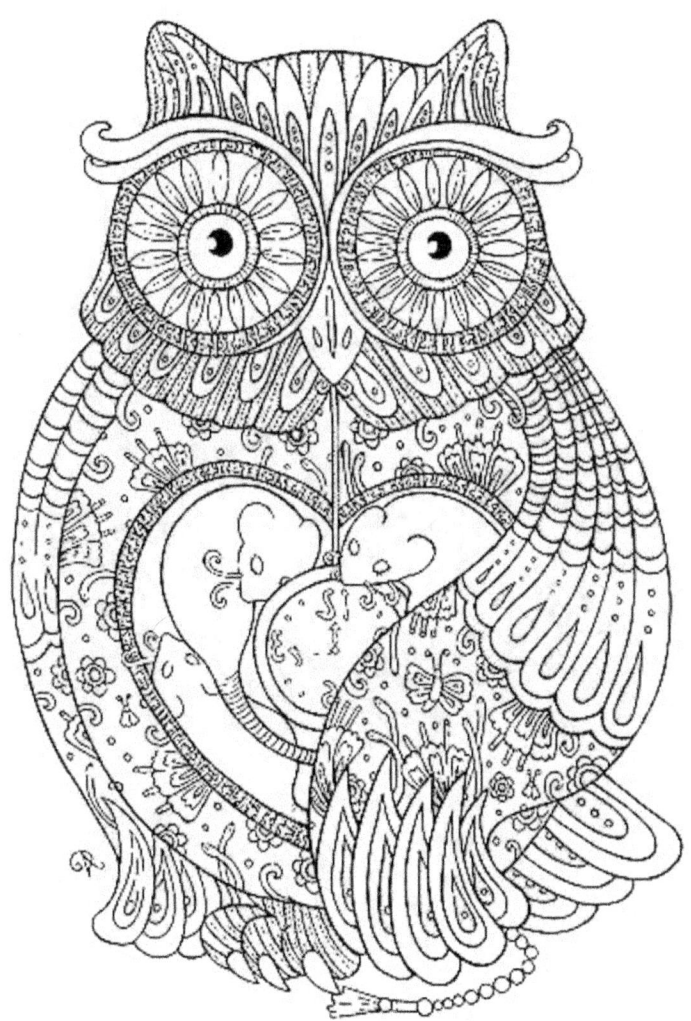

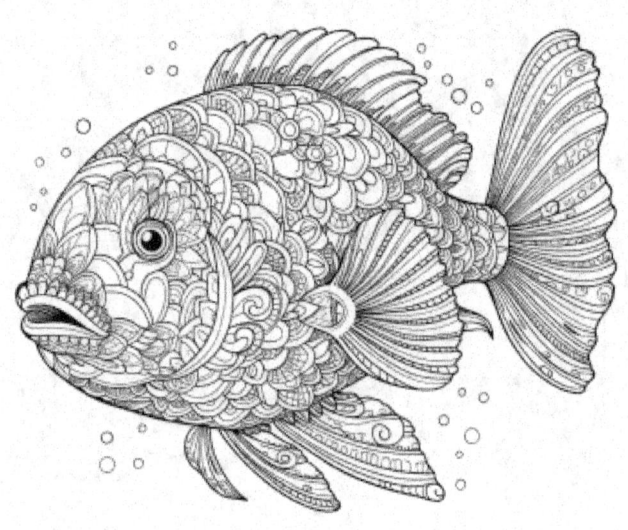

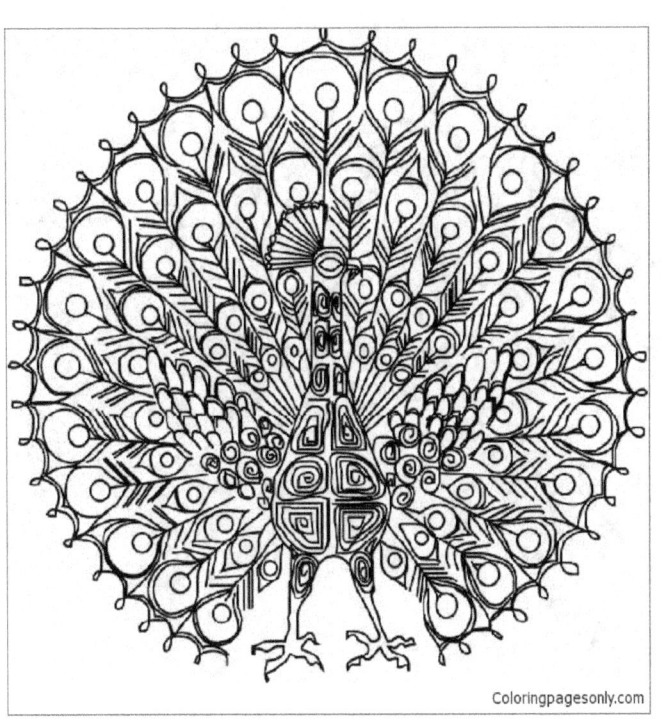

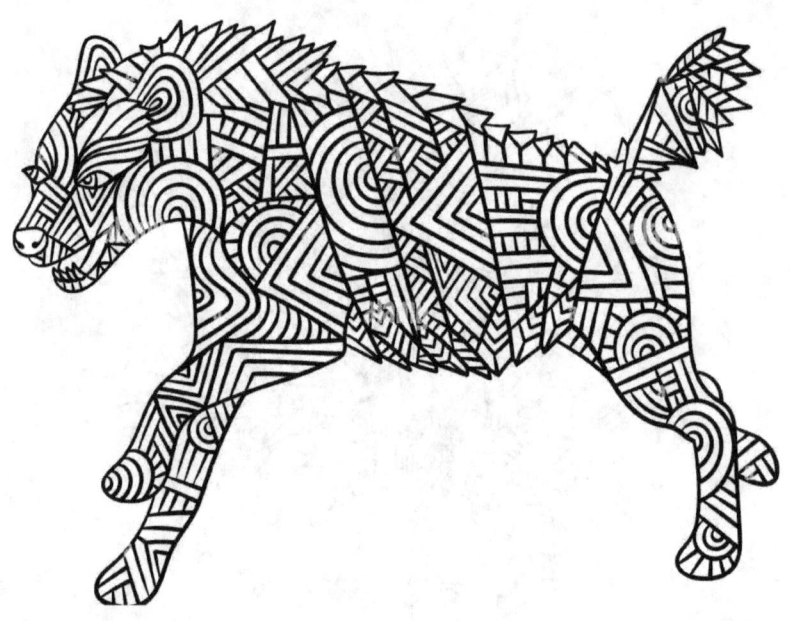

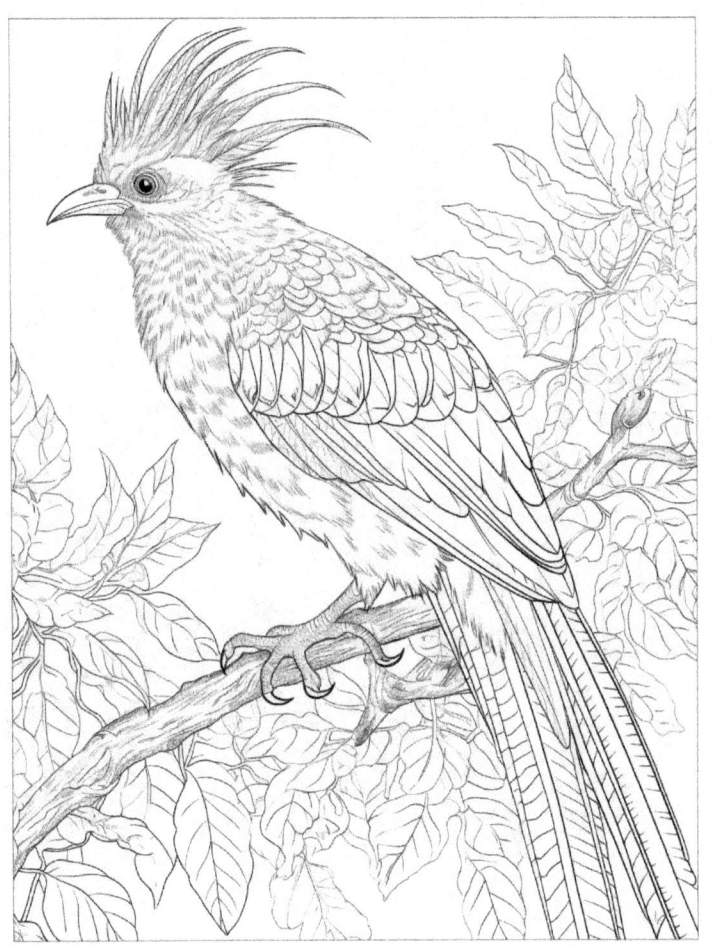

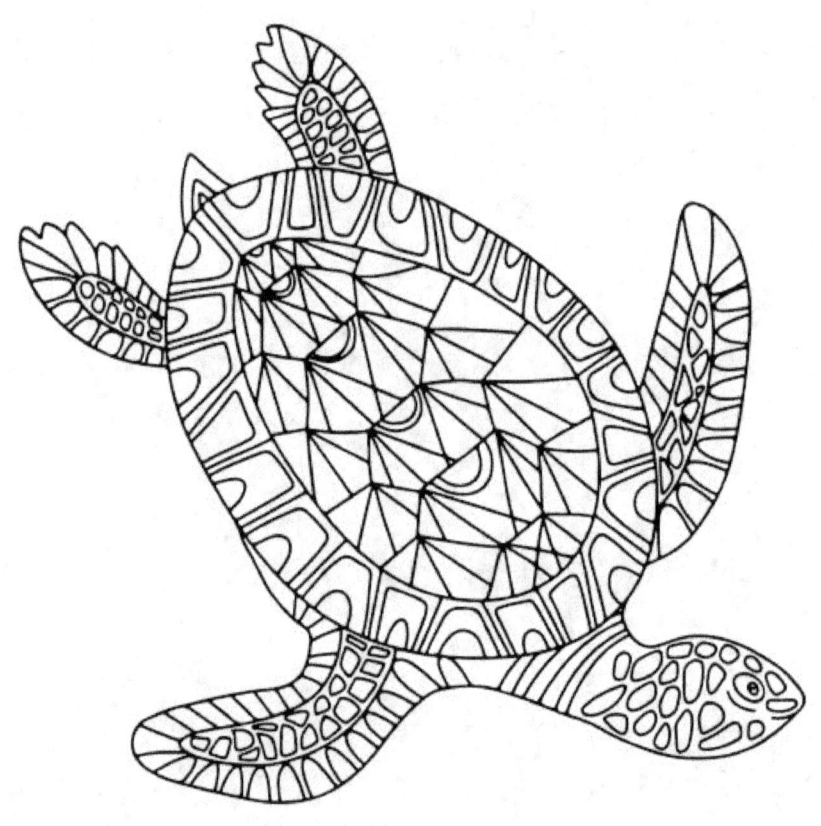

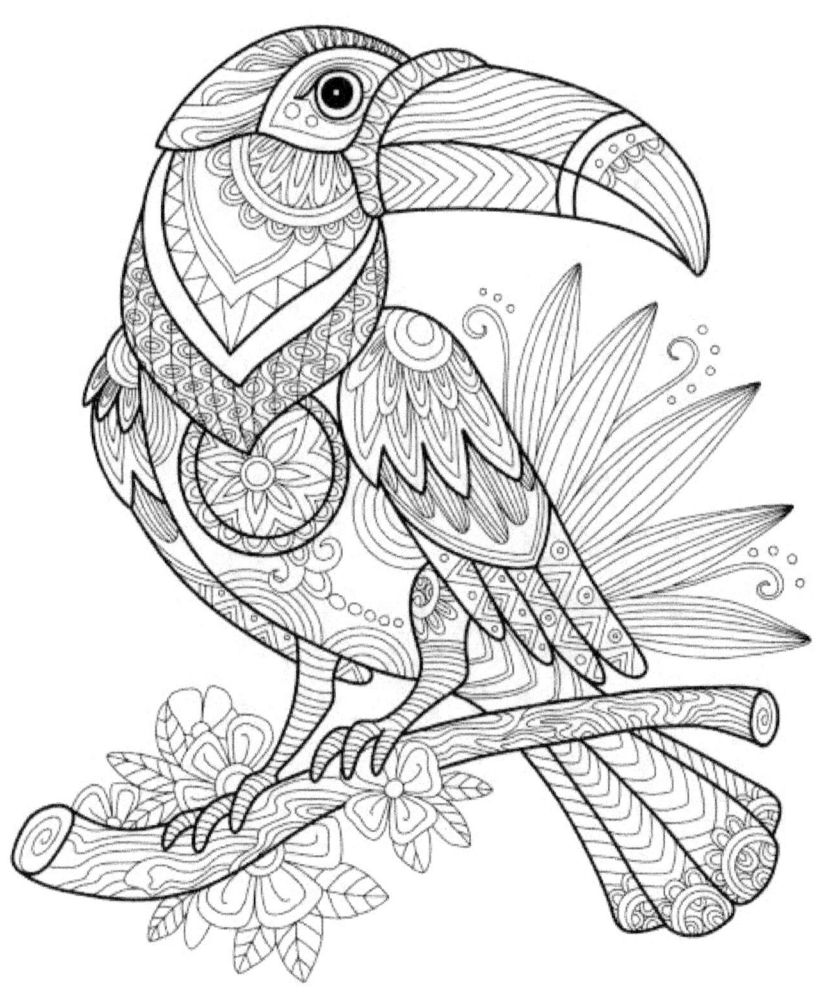

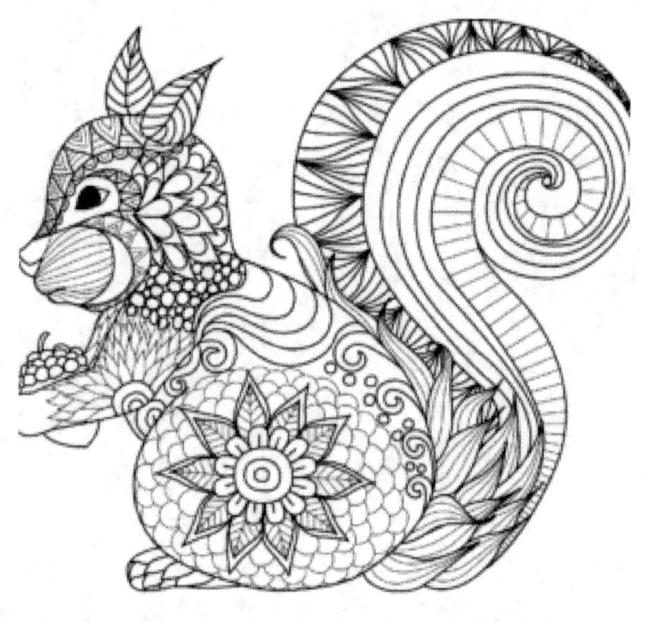

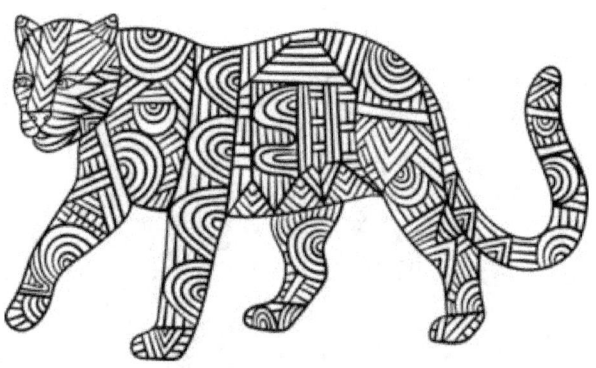

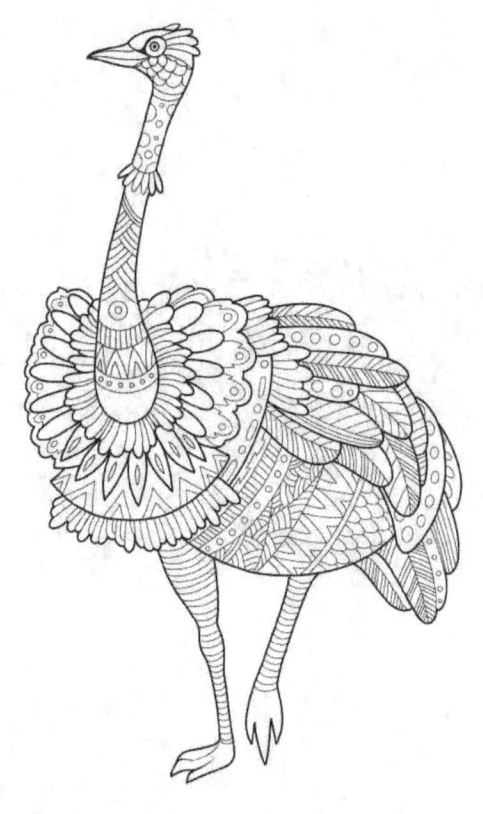

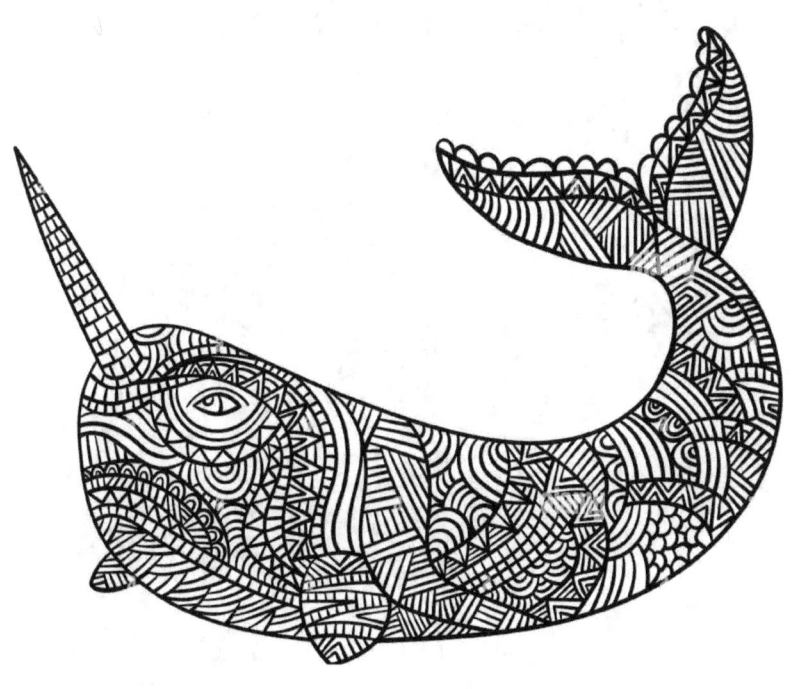

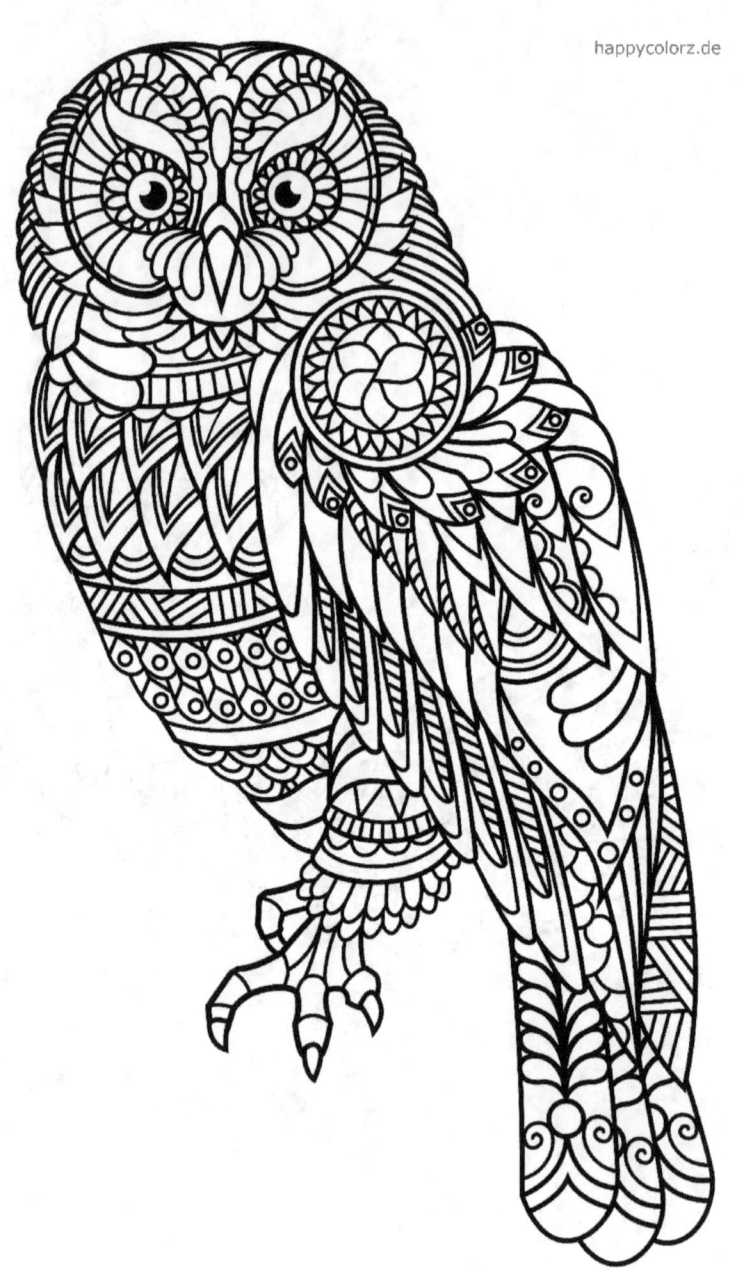

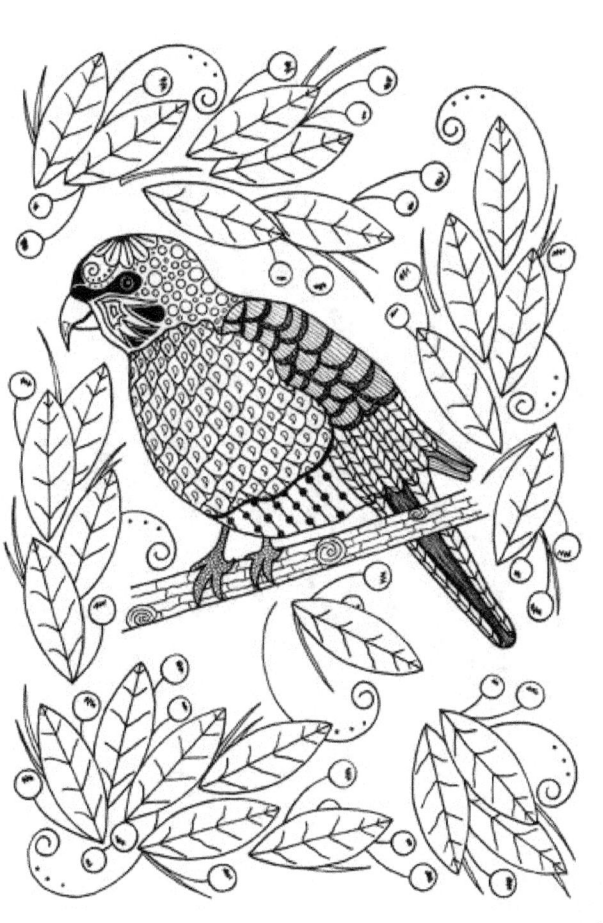

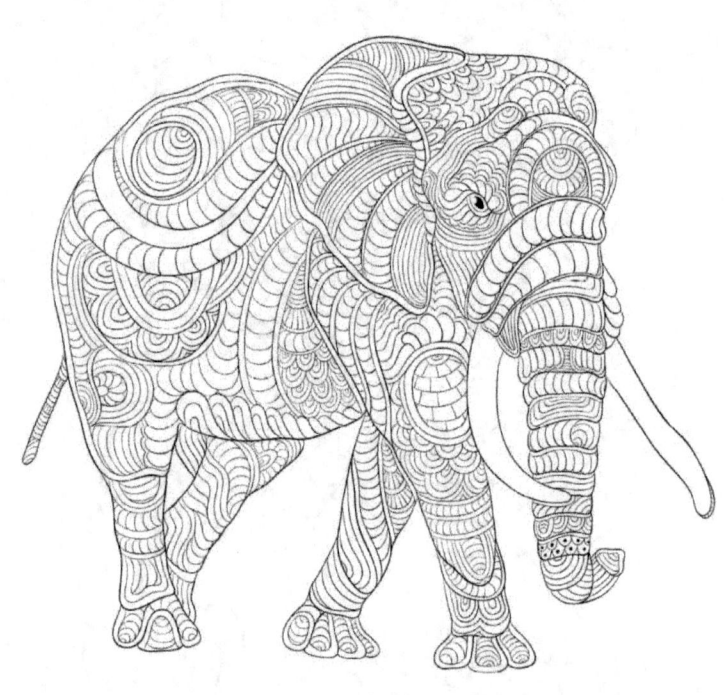

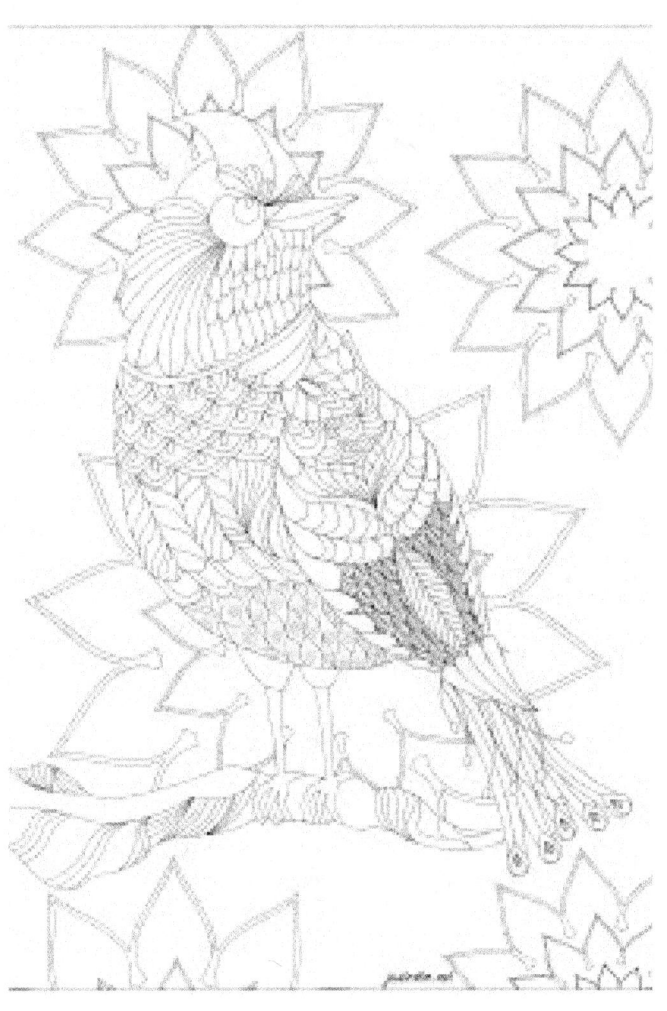

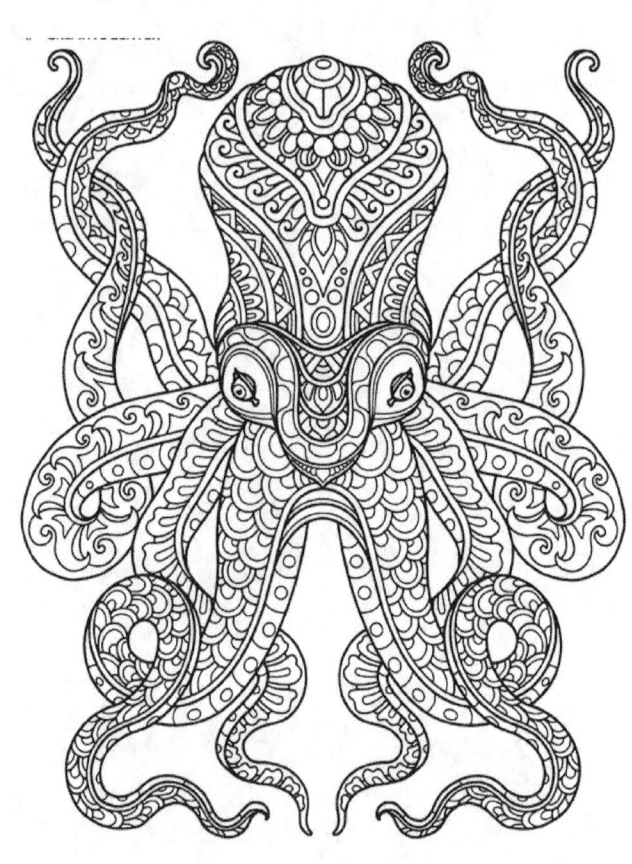

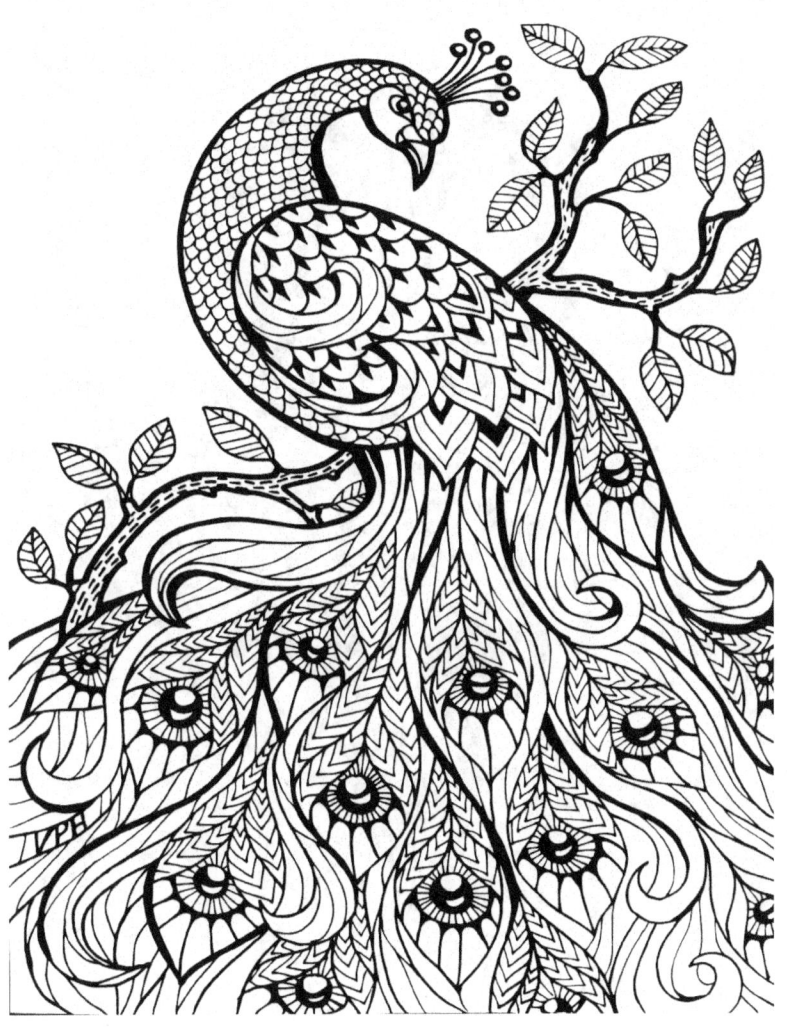

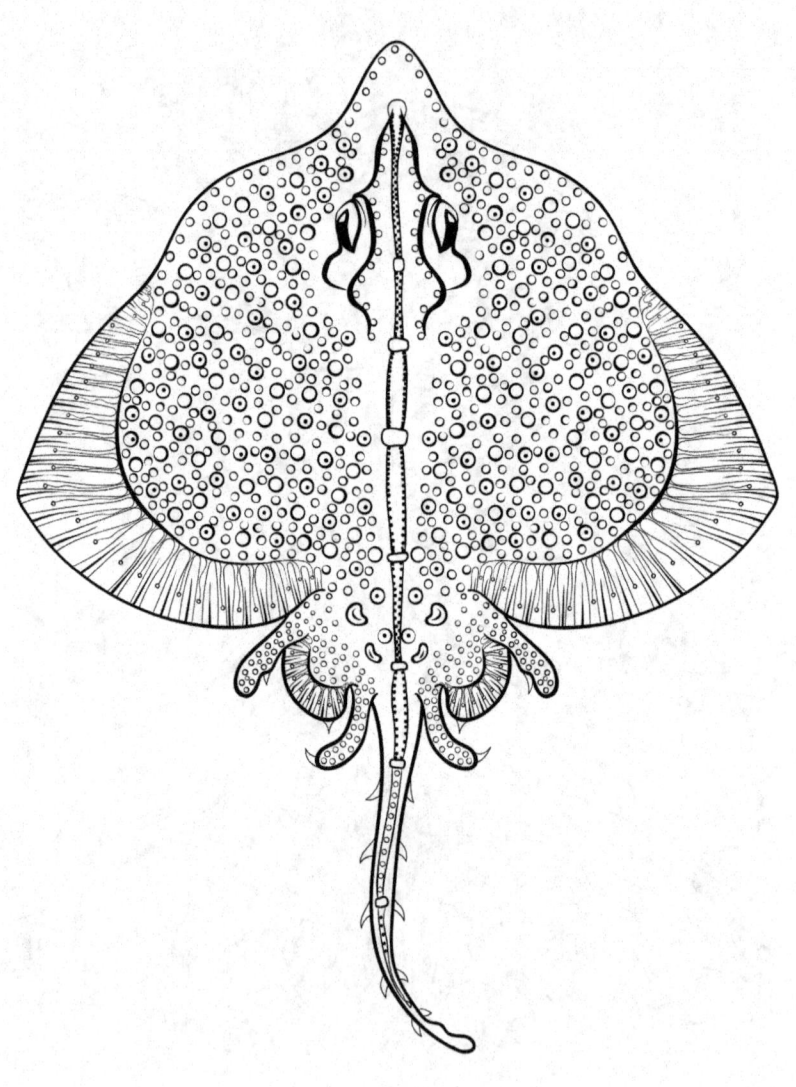

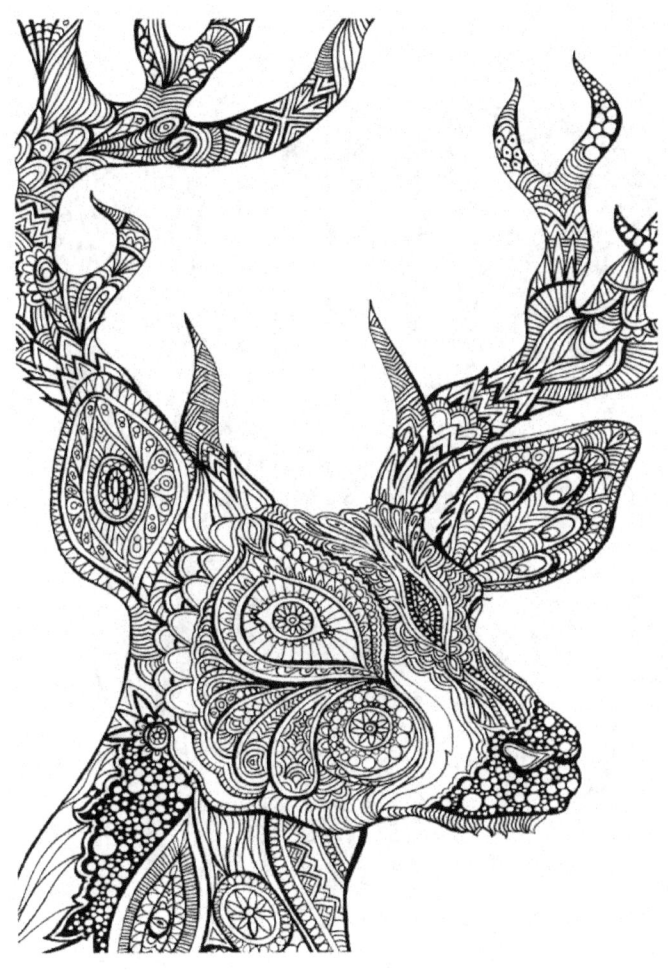

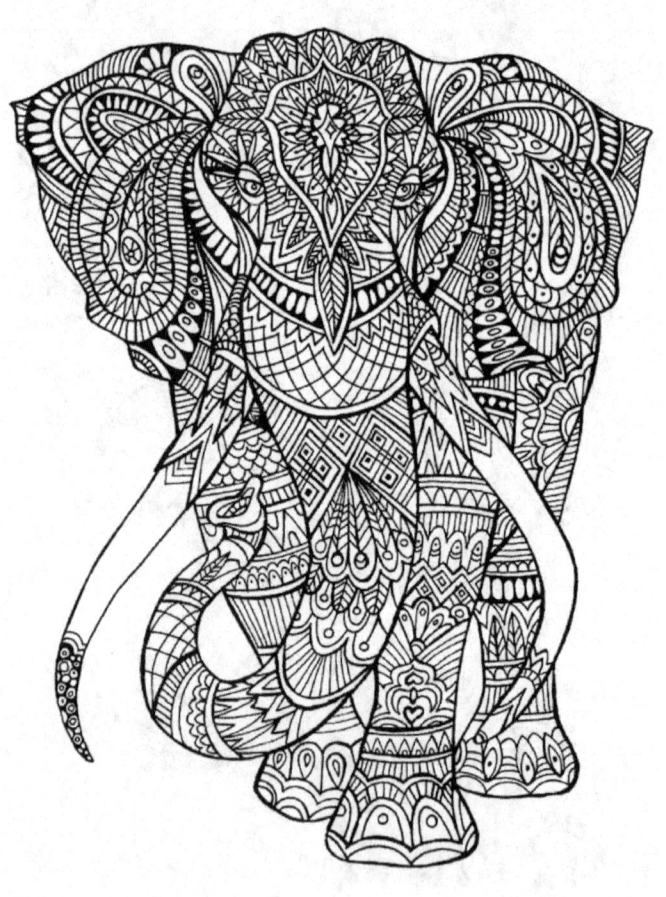

QUOTE FOR THE DAY

The essence of all beautiful art, all great art, is gratitude.

Friedrich Nietzsche

A picture is a poem without words.

Horace

Congrats!

....

....

You have just finished the Journey

www.ingramcontent.com/pod-product-compliance
Lightning Source LLC
Chambersburg PA
CBHW062258290526
45794CB00006B/2600